Manifesting the Life I Want

*JOURNAL FOR
VISION CASTING, CREATING & MANIFESTING*

Karema McGhee

I have the power to

design the life I want.

Copyright 2020 Karema McGhee - Companion Book for Psychological Ramblings of A Traveling Gypsy.

All rights reserved. No part of this book may be reproduced in any form or by electronic or mechanical means, including information storage and retrieval systems, without permission from the publisher, except by reviewers, who may quote brief passages in reviews.

Send all inquiries to luxinousbrand@gmail.com.

What is the law of attraction?

The belief that thoughts can attract things into our lives, good or bad, is simply the overall thought. This so-called New Age thought process is not New Age at all. In fact, there are a few Biblical references to what we call today the Law of Attraction.

Proverbs 23:7 "As a man thinks in his heart, so is he."

Matthew - 21:22 "And all things, whatsoever you shall ask in prayer, believing, you shall receive."

Mark - 11:24 "Therefore I tell you, whatever you ask for in prayer, believe that you have received it, and it will be yours."

It is clear that what we call New Age manifesting has been around much longer than we like to let on. The Bible has been clear on just how powerful your tongue is, and to further give you an example of the power you have here in this world, if you are a believer, he's given you dominion.

All you have to do is believe and ask.

The trouble though I see for many is getting them to work out all of the noise in their heads, getting rid of the toxic ways of thinking, of being, and of knowing. The hardest part for most people is undoing useless thought patterns. Useless mulling over of circumstances, about how things went and why. Many people spend much time going over playback and playthrough, not knowing that this energy is what actually attracts more of the same things. The things they don't want, they keep attracting because they keep thinking them.

My objective in this book is to get you to study the art of your thoughts, and to train your brain into a new way of thinking.

They say that learning comes by habituation, by way of repetition. This book is your journal for recreating the life you want, by having a safe space to write out the things you want in a repetitive manner. At some point, you'll hear your thoughts over and over again, so much so that your brain starts to believe what you are creating here in this manifestation bible. This action is called learning. Although un-learning is more fitting, we'll leave it there.

This is not a journal for things as they are. They have diaries for that. This is a journal for how you would want things to be. This journal is how you will start to visualize things as you would want them to become. You'll write out your ideas, your plans, your goals, dreams and desires. You'll look forward to vision casting, because manifestation is nothing but a vision you created in your mind's eye, that you were able to make a reality. Vision casting is pushing forward a vision.

Vision Casting Tips:

1. Before you begin writing or casting your vision forward, be sure to make sure your environment is clean and free of clutter.

2. Be sure to wash your body and decompress from the day. Especially if you had to work a job you would like to see changed, or if you had a day of negativity. To decompress from the stressful day, taking a bath before writing in your journal is a sure way to be relaxed before you create.

3. Get clear about your idea. Write a rough draft first. Rewrite it again, and again, and allow it to unfold.

4. Be sure to remember the rules of manifesting the life you want – the focus is not on things as they are, but as you would want them to be.

5. Remain positive in your writings. High vibrations are extremely important when you are trying to bring forth change. The higher your vibrations, the more positive space you are in, and the easier it is to bring forth your vision.

6. Do not be afraid to ask for what you want. Not just in this journal, but in everything going forward.

7. Allow your new life, or your new ideas of how you want your life to unfold. Allow it now. Feel it, see it, be it, on all levels.

8. Do not share with anyone your plans until they have manifested.

9. Do not share with anyone that you are working on manifesting your dreams or that you are working to recreate a new life for yourself. Keep these things private to reserve your energy.

10. Get excited about being blessed beyond measure. Look around you as things are and take stock in how great things are now. Gratitude moves the needle. Excitement brings it home.

2 Things to Change Before Manifesting

1. Things that stress you out
2. Things that make you feel less about who you are

It's important to realize that if you have friends and family in your life that bring havoc, pain, or add dysfunction, it's okay to distance yourself. Give yourself permission to remove your presence from anything, anyone and anyplace that is not serving the vision you have for your future.

If it's reading magazines that make you feel bad about your self-image, take a break. If it's the unrealistic images on social media, take a break. Give yourself a self-improvement time-out from anything not serving where you want to go. Give yourself a break, as you begin to create your breakthrough. Be serious about your plans and be unapologetic about what you require to clear your mind and to get you where you want to go.

Date: ....

Time: ....

Intention: ....

Vision Casting Ethics: I send forth my vision with pure love, faith and certainty. I know that my vision will return back to me; it will not return to be void. I send the energy forward with no harm or hurt to others.

_____

_____

_____

_____

_____

Date: ....

Time: ....

Intention: ....

Vision Casting Ethics: I send forth my vision with pure love, faith and certainty. I know that my vision will return back to me; it will not return to be void. I send the energy forward with no harm or hurt to others.

_____

_____

_____

_____

_____

Date: ....

Time: ....

Intention: ....

Vision Casting Ethics: I send forth my vision with pure love, faith and certainty. I know that my vision will return back to me; it will not return to be void. I send the energy forward with no harm or hurt to others.

_____

_____

_____

_____

_____

Date: . . . .

Time: . . . .

Intention: . . . .

Vision Casting Ethics: I send forth my vision with pure love, faith and certainty. I know that my vision will return back to me; it will not return to be void. I send the energy forward with no harm or hurt to others.

_____

_____

_____

_____

_____

Date: . . . .

Time: . . . .

Intention: . . . .

Vision Casting Ethics: I send forth my vision with pure love, faith and certainty. I know that my vision will return back to me; it will not return to be void. I send the energy forward with no harm or hurt to others.

_____

_____

_____

_____

_____

Date: ....

Time: ....

Intention: ....

Vision Casting Ethics: I send forth my vision with pure love, faith and certainty. I know that my vision will return back to me; it will not return to be void. I send the energy forward with no harm or hurt to others.

_____

_____

_____

_____

_____

Date: ....

Time: ....

Intention: ....

Vision Casting Ethics: I send forth my vision with pure love, faith and certainty. I know that my vision will return back to me; it will not return to be void. I send the energy forward with no harm or hurt to others.

_____

_____

_____

_____

_____

Date: ....

Time: ....

Intention: ....

Vision Casting Ethics: I send forth my vision with pure love, faith and certainty. I know that my vision will return back to me; it will not return to be void. I send the energy forward with no harm or hurt to others.

_____

_____

_____

_____

_____

Date: . . . .

Time: . . . .

Intention: . . . .

Vision Casting Ethics: I send forth my vision with pure love, faith and certainty. I know that my vision will return back to me; it will not return to be void. I send the energy forward with no harm or hurt to others.

Date: ....

Time: ....

Intention: ....

Vision Casting Ethics: I send forth my vision with pure love, faith and certainty. I know that my vision will return back to me; it will not return to be void. I send the energy forward with no harm or hurt to others.

_____

_____

_____

_____

_____

Date: ....

Time: ....

Intention: ....

Vision Casting Ethics: I send forth my vision with pure love, faith and certainty. I know that my vision will return back to me; it will not return to be void. I send the energy forward with no harm or hurt to others.

_____

_____

_____

_____

_____

Date: ....

Time: ....

Intention: ....

Vision Casting Ethics: I send forth my vision with pure love, faith and certainty. I know that my vision will return back to me; it will not return to be void. I send the energy forward with no harm or hurt to others.

_____

_____

_____

_____

_____

Date: ....

Time: ....

Intention: ....

Vision Casting Ethics: I send forth my vision with pure love, faith and certainty. I know that my vision will return back to me; it will not return to be void. I send the energy forward with no harm or hurt to others.

_____

_____

_____

_____

_____

Date: ....

Time: ....

Intention: ....

Vision Casting Ethics: I send forth my vision with pure love, faith and certainty. I know that my vision will return back to me; it will not return to be void. I send the energy forward with no harm or hurt to others.

Date: ....

Time: ....

Intention: ....

Vision Casting Ethics: I send forth my vision with pure love, faith and certainty. I know that my vision will return back to me; it will not return to be void. I send the energy forward with no harm or hurt to others.

_____

_____

_____

_____

_____

_____

Date: . . . .

Time: . . . .

Intention: . . . .

Vision Casting Ethics: I send forth my vision with pure love, faith and certainty. I know that my vision will return back to me; it will not return to be void. I send the energy forward with no harm or hurt to others.

_____

_____

_____

_____

_____

Date: ....

Time: ....

Intention: ....

Vision Casting Ethics: I send forth my vision with pure love, faith and certainty. I know that my vision will return back to me; it will not return to be void. I send the energy forward with no harm or hurt to others.

_____

_____

_____

_____

_____

Date: ....

Time: ....

Intention: ....

Vision Casting Ethics: I send forth my vision with pure love, faith and certainty. I know that my vision will return back to me; it will not return to be void. I send the energy forward with no harm or hurt to others.

_____

_____

_____

_____

_____

Date: . . . .

Time: . . . .

Intention: . . . .

Vision Casting Ethics: I send forth my vision with pure love, faith and certainty. I know that my vision will return back to me; it will not return to be void. I send the energy forward with no harm or hurt to others.

_____

_____

_____

_____

_____

_____

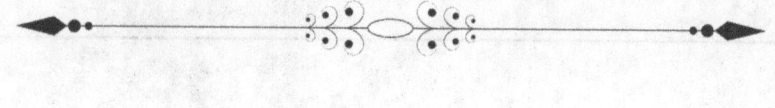

Date: . . . .

Time: . . . .

Intention: . . . .

Vision Casting Ethics: I send forth my vision with pure love, faith and certainty. I know that my vision will return back to me; it will not return to be void. I send the energy forward with no harm or hurt to others.

_____

_____

_____

_____

_____

Date: . . . .

Time: . . . .

Intention: . . . .

Vision Casting Ethics: I send forth my vision with pure love, faith and certainty. I know that my vision will return back to me; it will not return to be void. I send the energy forward with no harm or hurt to others.

_____

_____

_____

_____

_____

Date: . . . .

Time: . . . .

Intention: . . . .

Vision Casting Ethics: I send forth my vision with pure love, faith and certainty. I know that my vision will return back to me; it will not return to be void. I send the energy forward with no harm or hurt to others.

_____

_____

_____

_____

_____

_____

Date: . . . .

Time: . . . .

Intention: . . . .

Vision Casting Ethics: I send forth my vision with pure love, faith and certainty. I know that my vision will return back to me; it will not return to be void. I send the energy forward with no harm or hurt to others.

_____

_____

_____

_____

_____

Date: ....

Time: ....

Intention: ....

Vision Casting Ethics: I send forth my vision with pure love, faith and certainty. I know that my vision will return back to me; it will not return to be void. I send the energy forward with no harm or hurt to others.

_____

_____

_____

_____

_____

Date: ....

Time: ....

Intention: ....

Vision Casting Ethics: I send forth my vision with pure love, faith and certainty. I know that my vision will return back to me; it will not return to be void. I send the energy forward with no harm or hurt to others.

_____

_____

_____

_____

_____

Date: ....

Time: ....

Intention: ....

Vision Casting Ethics: I send forth my vision with pure love, faith and certainty. I know that my vision will return back to me; it will not return to be void. I send the energy forward with no harm or hurt to others.

_____

_____

_____

_____

_____

Date: ....

Time: ....

Intention: ....

Vision Casting Ethics: I send forth my vision with pure love, faith and certainty. I know that my vision will return back to me; it will not return to be void. I send the energy forward with no harm or hurt to others.

_____

_____

_____

_____

_____

Date: ....

Time: ....

Intention: ....

Vision Casting Ethics: I send forth my vision with pure love, faith and certainty. I know that my vision will return back to me; it will not return to be void. I send the energy forward with no harm or hurt to others.

_____

_____

_____

_____

_____

Date: ....

Time: ....

Intention: ....

Vision Casting Ethics: I send forth my vision with pure love, faith and certainty. I know that my vision will return back to me; it will not return to be void. I send the energy forward with no harm or hurt to others.

_____

_____

_____

_____

_____

Date: . . . .

Time: . . . .

Intention: . . . .

Vision Casting Ethics: I send forth my vision with pure love, faith and certainty. I know that my vision will return back to me; it will not return to be void. I send the energy forward with no harm or hurt to others.

_____

_____

_____

_____

_____

Date: ....

Time: ....

Intention: ....

Vision Casting Ethics: I send forth my vision with pure love, faith and certainty. I know that my vision will return back to me; it will not return to be void. I send the energy forward with no harm or hurt to others.

_____

_____

_____

_____

_____

Date: ....

Time: ....

Intention: ....

Vision Casting Ethics: I send forth my vision with pure love, faith and certainty. I know that my vision will return back to me; it will not return to be void. I send the energy forward with no harm or hurt to others.

_____

_____

_____

_____

_____

Date: ....

Time: ....

Intention: ....

Vision Casting Ethics: I send forth my vision with pure love, faith and certainty. I know that my vision will return back to me; it will not return to be void. I send the energy forward with no harm or hurt to others.

_____

_____

_____

_____

_____

_____

Date: ....

Time: ....

Intention: ....

Vision Casting Ethics: I send forth my vision with pure love, faith and certainty. I know that my vision will return back to me; it will not return to be void. I send the energy forward with no harm or hurt to others.

_____

_____

_____

_____

_____

Date: ....

Time: ....

Intention: ....

Vision Casting Ethics: I send forth my vision with pure love, faith and certainty. I know that my vision will return back to me; it will not return to be void. I send the energy forward with no harm or hurt to others.

_____

_____

_____

_____

_____

Date: ……………………………

Time: ……………………………

Intention: …………………………

Vision Casting Ethics: I send forth my vision with pure love, faith and certainty. I know that my vision will return back to me; it will not return to be void. I send the energy forward with no harm or hurt to others.

_____

_____

_____

_____

_____

_____

Date: ....

Time: ....

Intention: ....

Vision Casting Ethics: I send forth my vision with pure love, faith and certainty. I know that my vision will return back to me; it will not return to be void. I send the energy forward with no harm or hurt to others.

_____

_____

_____

_____

_____

Date: . . . .

Time: . . . .

Intention: . . . .

Vision Casting Ethics: I send forth my vision with pure love, faith and certainty. I know that my vision will return back to me; it will not return to be void. I send the energy forward with no harm or hurt to others.

_____

_____

_____

_____

_____

Date: . . . .

Time: . . . .

Intention: . . . .

Vision Casting Ethics: I send forth my vision with pure love, faith and certainty. I know that my vision will return back to me; it will not return to be void. I send the energy forward with no harm or hurt to others.

_____

_____

_____

_____

_____

Date: . . . .

Time: . . . .

Intention: . . . .

Vision Casting Ethics: I send forth my vision with pure love, faith and certainty. I know that my vision will return back to me; it will not return to be void. I send the energy forward with no harm or hurt to others.

_____

_____

_____

_____

_____

_____

Date: ....

Time: ....

Intention: ....

Vision Casting Ethics: I send forth my vision with pure love, faith and certainty. I know that my vision will return back to me; it will not return to be void. I send the energy forward with no harm or hurt to others.

_____

_____

_____

_____

_____

Date: ....

Time: ....

Intention: ....

Vision Casting Ethics: I send forth my vision with pure love, faith and certainty. I know that my vision will return back to me; it will not return to be void. I send the energy forward with no harm or hurt to others.

_____

_____

_____

_____

_____

Date: . . . .

Time: . . . .

Intention: . . . .

Vision Casting Ethics: I send forth my vision with pure love, faith and certainty. I know that my vision will return back to me; it will not return to be void. I send the energy forward with no harm or hurt to others.

_____

_____

_____

_____

_____

_____

Date: ....

Time: ....

Intention: ....

Vision Casting Ethics: I send forth my vision with pure love, faith and certainty. I know that my vision will return back to me; it will not return to be void. I send the energy forward with no harm or hurt to others.

_____

_____

_____

_____

_____

Date: ....

Time: ....

Intention: ....

Vision Casting Ethics: I send forth my vision with pure love, faith and certainty. I know that my vision will return back to me; it will not return to be void. I send the energy forward with no harm or hurt to others.

_____

_____

_____

_____

_____

Date: ....

Time: ....

Intention: ....

Vision Casting Ethics: I send forth my vision with pure love, faith and certainty. I know that my vision will return back to me; it will not return to be void. I send the energy forward with no harm or hurt to others.

_____

_____

_____

_____

_____

Date: . . . .

Time: . . . .

Intention: . . . .

Vision Casting Ethics: I send forth my vision with pure love, faith and certainty. I know that my vision will return back to me; it will not return to be void. I send the energy forward with no harm or hurt to others.

_____

_____

_____

_____

_____

Date: . . . .

Time: . . . .

Intention: . . . .

Vision Casting Ethics: I send forth my vision with pure love, faith and certainty. I know that my vision will return back to me; it will not return to be void. I send the energy forward with no harm or hurt to others.

_____

_____

_____

_____

_____

_____

Date: ....

Time: ....

Intention: ....

Vision Casting Ethics: I send forth my vision with pure love, faith and certainty. I know that my vision will return back to me; it will not return to be void. I send the energy forward with no harm or hurt to others.

_____

_____

_____

_____

_____

_____

Date: ....

Time: ....

Intention: ....

Vision Casting Ethics: I send forth my vision with pure love, faith and certainty. I know that my vision will return back to me; it will not return to be void. I send the energy forward with no harm or hurt to others.

_____

_____

_____

_____

_____

Date: ....

Time: ....

Intention: ....

Vision Casting Ethics: I send forth my vision with pure love, faith and certainty. I know that my vision will return back to me; it will not return to be void. I send the energy forward with no harm or hurt to others.

_____

_____

_____

_____

_____

Date: . . . .

Time: . . . .

Intention: . . . .

Vision Casting Ethics: I send forth my vision with pure love, faith and certainty. I know that my vision will return back to me; it will not return to be void. I send the energy forward with no harm or hurt to others.

_____

_____

_____

_____

_____

Date: ....

Time: ....

Intention: ....

Vision Casting Ethics: I send forth my vision with pure love, faith and certainty. I know that my vision will return back to me; it will not return to be void. I send the energy forward with no harm or hurt to others.

_____

_____

_____

_____

_____

Date: . . . .

Time: . . . .

Intention: . . . .

Vision Casting Ethics: I send forth my vision with pure love, faith and certainty. I know that my vision will return back to me; it will not return to be void. I send the energy forward with no harm or hurt to others.

_____

_____

_____

_____

_____

Date: . . . .

Time: . . . .

Intention: . . . .

Vision Casting Ethics: I send forth my vision with pure love, faith and certainty. I know that my vision will return back to me; it will not return to be void. I send the energy forward with no harm or hurt to others.

_____

_____

_____

_____

_____

Date: . . . .

Time: . . . .

Intention: . . . .

Vision Casting Ethics: I send forth my vision with pure love, faith and certainty. I know that my vision will return back to me; it will not return to be void. I send the energy forward with no harm or hurt to others.

Date: . . . .

Time: . . . .

Intention: . . . .

Vision Casting Ethics: I send forth my vision with pure love, faith and certainty. I know that my vision will return back to me; it will not return to be void. I send the energy forward with no harm or hurt to others.

_____

_____

_____

_____

_____

Date: . . . .

Time: . . . .

Intention: . . . .

Vision Casting Ethics: I send forth my vision with pure love, faith and certainty. I know that my vision will return back to me; it will not return to be void. I send the energy forward with no harm or hurt to others.

_____

_____

_____

_____

_____

_____

Date: . . . .

Time: . . . .

Intention: . . . .

Vision Casting Ethics: I send forth my vision with pure love, faith and certainty. I know that my vision will return back to me; it will not return to be void. I send the energy forward with no harm or hurt to others.

_____

_____

_____

_____

_____

Date: . . . .

Time: . . . .

Intention: . . . .

Vision Casting Ethics: I send forth my vision with pure love, faith and certainty. I know that my vision will return back to me; it will not return to be void. I send the energy forward with no harm or hurt to others.

_____

_____

_____

_____

_____

Date: ....

Time: ....

Intention: ....

Vision Casting Ethics: I send forth my vision with pure love, faith and certainty. I know that my vision will return back to me; it will not return to be void. I send the energy forward with no harm or hurt to others.

_____

_____

_____

_____

_____

Date: . . . .

Time: . . . .

Intention: . . . .

Vision Casting Ethics: I send forth my vision with pure love, faith and certainty. I know that my vision will return back to me; it will not return to be void. I send the energy forward with no harm or hurt to others.

_____

_____

_____

_____

_____

Date: . . . .

Time: . . . .

Intention: . . . .

Vision Casting Ethics: I send forth my vision with pure love, faith and certainty. I know that my vision will return back to me; it will not return to be void. I send the energy forward with no harm or hurt to others.

_____

_____

_____

_____

_____

_____

Date: ....

Time: ....

Intention: ....

Vision Casting Ethics: I send forth my vision with pure love, faith and certainty. I know that my vision will return back to me; it will not return to be void. I send the energy forward with no harm or hurt to others.

_____

_____

_____

_____

_____

Date: . . . .

Time: . . . .

Intention: . . . .

Vision Casting Ethics: I send forth my vision with pure love, faith and certainty. I know that my vision will return back to me; it will not return to be void. I send the energy forward with no harm or hurt to others.

_____

_____

_____

_____

_____

Date: . . . .

Time: . . . .

Intention: . . . .

Vision Casting Ethics: I send forth my vision with pure love, faith and certainty. I know that my vision will return back to me; it will not return to be void. I send the energy forward with no harm or hurt to others.

Date: . . . .

Time: . . . .

Intention: . . . .

Vision Casting Ethics: I send forth my vision with pure love, faith and certainty. I know that my vision will return back to me; it will not return to be void. I send the energy forward with no harm or hurt to others.

_____

_____

_____

_____

_____

_____

Date: ....

Time: ....

Intention: ....

Vision Casting Ethics: I send forth my vision with pure love, faith and certainty. I know that my vision will return back to me; it will not return to be void. I send the energy forward with no harm or hurt to others.

_____

_____

_____

_____

_____

Date: . . . .

Time: . . . .

Intention: . . . .

Vision Casting Ethics: I send forth my vision with pure love, faith and certainty. I know that my vision will return back to me; it will not return to be void. I send the energy forward with no harm or hurt to others.

_____

_____

_____

_____

_____

_____

Date: ....

Time: ....

Intention: ....

Vision Casting Ethics: I send forth my vision with pure love, faith and certainty. I know that my vision will return back to me; it will not return to be void. I send the energy forward with no harm or hurt to others.

_____

_____

_____

_____

_____

www.ingramcontent.com/pod-product-compliance
Lightning Source LLC
Chambersburg PA
CBHW011315080526
44587CB00024B/4007